ONLY IN AMERICA

ONLY

IN

AMERICA

SOME UNEXPECTED SCENERY

David Graham

Introduction by Jane and Michael Stern

Alfred A. Knopf
New York
1991

This Is a Borzoi Book Published by Alfred A. Knopf, Inc.

Copyright ©1991 by David Graham

Introduction copyright ©1991 by Jane and Michael Stern

All rights reserved under International and Pan-American Copyright Conventions. Published in the United States by Alfred A. Knopf, Inc., New York, and simultaneously in Canada by Random House of Canada Limited, Toronto. Distributed by Random House, Inc., New York.

Library of Congress Cataloging-in-Publication Data

Graham, David [date]

Only in America : some unexpected scenery / David Graham ; introduction by Jane and Michael Stern.—1st ed.

p.   cm.

ISBN 0–394–58215–2

1. United States—Description and travel—1981– —Views.

2. Landscape—United States—Pictorial works. I. Title.

E169.04.G733   1991

973.92'022'2—dc20   90–52913   CIP

Manufactured in the United States of America

Published September 26, 1991

Second Printing, December 1991

To Dory

Thank you for letting me take these pictures
between playgrounds. I hope that they will
help you to remember when you were little.

Acknowledgments

It seems inevitable that one should have to thank a variety of people at the end of a book. This time, the second time I've reached the end of a book, it seems particularly miraculous that the world conspired to let me take the necessary pictures.

The first evidence of perfect worldly cooperation came with Victoria Wilson's support at Alfred A. Knopf. I am extremely grateful for her understanding.

In the actual making of the photographs, I could not have anticipated the selfless and generous nature of Gene Kennedy, a great photographer in his own right. On four separate occasions, Gene drove a ridiculous distance to pick me up at some arbitrary airport. As if this weren't enough, he would then act as my chauffeur, tour guide, and companion, making almost all my needs his first priority. I can't thank him enough, especially for when I *wasn't* there to be helped.

As always, my wife, Jeannine Vannais, is to be thanked for telling me to go and photograph, even when it meant stranding her, repeatedly, as I took off with Gene.

Lastly, for those times when we were traveling as a family unit, I would like to thank my daughter, Dory, for a tour of the playgrounds of the eastern United States.

Introduction

Eureka! David Graham has found something we have been looking for for a long time. He found America. He took some pictures of it, and it is a good thing he did, because what he saw is so astonishing that none of us would believe it if we couldn't see it with our own eyes. In a way, everything in this book's pictures is familiar; if you have ever motored out a two-lane beyond the city limits, you have likely glimpsed many of the kinds of places and scenes that David Graham saw. But whoa! How did it all get so strange? You never saw the roadside quite like this, except maybe in a dream in which everything was in your face with perturbing vim, brighter than in real life. Even an audacious surrealist might not have the nerve to create such vistas out of whole cloth, but David Graham gets them in his view-finder and devises a perspective that turns what most of us obliviously cruise past into a magical landscape.

You could describe *Only in America* as a book of photographs of sights along such well-worn highways as 301 through the Carolinas and 89A in New Mexico and the remains of 66 in Oklahoma. But when you look at these pictures, you are not looking at snapshots of simply interesting or even picturesque scenes. This is scenery made fabulous. A row of drab utility sheds in front of a row of undistinguished grain elevators becomes an enthralling vista. A giant male torso on a billboard appears to be more excruciatingly nude than any body ought to be. Colossal arrows from God-knows-where poke into barren earth with utmost urgency. These pictures are not scenery; they are mise-en-scènes, and they plumb the spirit of the American road.

David Graham has a way of putting things together in a picture that makes your jaw drop. The back of a foam resin dinosaur, the front of a semi, and two snow tires are assembled in one photo with stunning pictorial dynamics: the bulbous hood of the truck and the flanks of the dino are deliciously sensuous next to the jagged grooves in the hard rubber tires and the scruffy grass field where they have all been discarded. The neck of the great monster stretches so far back it seems to vanish headless into the sky. The strength of the image becomes a sign of abandonment far more compelling than tires, a broken-down truck, or a retired amusement-park brontosaur ever is. Likewise, a photograph of a huge, helium-filled float strapped down to the pavement the night before the Thanksgiving Day parade contains a frightful hobbled energy that the float will never have when it is unfurled in the daylight.

Every image in this book takes the form of an enigma, but nothing in this outlandish America appears photographically contrived. Flip through the pictures and gasp and laugh at what you see, and you will ask, *Is this for real?* Or in the words of the ever-popular paper place-mat puzzle in the booths of roadside beaneries: *What is wrong with this picture?* The answer is that there is nothing wrong with these pictures; the subjects in them are indeed for real. If contemplating the uncanny images David Graham has created and collected makes you giddy or sometimes even a little queasy at just how strange the landscape is, don't worry: there is nothing here that a couple of aspirins, a Di-Gel, a pair of dark Ray-Bans, and a fast V-8 convertible to get you on your way won't fix. Here, for better and for worse, in sickness and in health, is a nation of endless highways, cluttered roadsides, and overwhelming oddness just around the next bend.

It's a funny thing about America: people always seem to be out looking for it. Writers, folk singers, and photographers hunt high and low for the meaning and essence of it, especially along the highways, where they can feel the velocity that apparently makes us antsy Americans different than people in other, mellower places. When you are on the road, doing sixty or better, the sights are always whizzing past, and always different; so even if they are commonplace, they never have a chance to get too boring. The blur of the roadside, with all its advertising hype and buildings rising out of the desert and rusty automobile graveyards and fading signs for discontinued products and decrepit sleep-in-a-tepee motels and abandoned parade floats, is an archaeologist's paradise. As we looked through David Graham's book of pictures for the first time, we thought that we were seeing the remains of a bizarre yet painfully familiar civilization.

Some people drive past old diners and dilapidated dinosaur parks going somewhere else, or wishing they were passing something pretty like the Grand Canyon or the Smoky Mountains. There are no pretty pictures of the Grand Canyon or the Smoky Mountains or any of America's natural wonders in this book. David Graham doesn't seem interested in stopping to contemplate nature; what draws his attention are the urgencies of American civilization, a loopy spectacle of passions and advertising promises, where everyone wants to be noticed and everything has been created to look as big and important as possible. His photographs show hopes on the way up or down; his America is full of forty-foot-high guarantees from billboard con artists, disintegrating remains of tourist attractions that went bust last year or decades ago, and dreamers in aluminum-sided manufactured homes surrounded by their Jesus statues.

You can see what you want and make what you will out of this land's cluttered panorama of trash and oddments. Writers have been on the case since Alexis de Tocqueville, up through Jack Kerouac and Ken Kesey, William Least Heat Moon, and Calvin Trillin; and photographers have looked at it with such diverse points of view as those of Robert Frank, Diane Arbus, Elliot Erwitt, and Bill Eggleston. Having traveled a few blue highways ourselves and taken thousands of pictures of the things we have seen, we tip our hats to David Graham for his marvelous powers of sight. Pictures this eloquent don't just appear in front of a camera.

We can tell you this with certainty: Even if you get off the interstate and mosey into the weirdest places you can find and take pictures of every oddball character and kooky sign you see, it is hard to come up with a genuine and affecting portrait of this improbable country. It is difficult to go looking for the real America because America is so shifty. Just when you think you've got it figured out, it gives you the slip, like the winking-eye souvenir postcard we bought of Richard and Pat Nixon standing in front of the Capitol Dome. As you look at the picture and move your head from side to side, the former president and his lovely wife gleefully blink in tandem at the results of the election of 1972, as throngs of Lilliputian admirers half their size wave joyously in the background. Like the expression on Tricky Dick's face in that picture—one moment bright-eyed and eager, the next slit-eyed and cunning—America's expression changes as you watch it, especially as you travel past it on the highways. Look at the pictures in this book and you see a roadside that is always winking, then slithering out of comprehension. It is hokum, but there is enchantment in it, even when it is ridiculously ordinary—*especially* when it is ordinary.

Although he includes no familiar landmarks or famous national shrines, it is throbbingly clear which country David Graham has photographed. Only in America do you find such extremism and a landscape where nearly everything is too big, too bright, and too loud. Taken together these images are a portrait of a people who crave to be grand, and almost always succeed in being at least grandiose. It is a rendering of American roadlore, which like this country's folklore, is full of bluff and vulgarity, cheap thrills, sentiment, and the promise of perfect happiness: *Turn the desert into dream homes! Buy now, pay later! Jesus saves!* David Graham has created a national photo album that renders a brave and preposterous side of a country that never fears to be ridiculous in its quest for the sublime.

—JANE AND MICHAEL STERN

Only in America

Silos and Utility Sheds, Maumee, Ohio, 1988

3

Betty at Valvo's Candy and Gift Shop near Niagara Falls, New York, 1989
Betty was rescued from what appeared to be her final resting place
against a cliff in Butler County, Pennsylvania.

B-52, Orlando International Airport, Orlando, Florida, 1989

6   C & S Body and Fender Shop, Las Vegas, Nevada, 1989

The Center of the World, Felicity, California, 1986
On May 21, 1985, this spot was legally established as the Official Center of the World. Shortly after that, the town of Felicity was created. These gestures resulted from a children's book, *Coe the Good Dragon at the Center of the World,* written by Jacques-Andre Istel, the mayor of Felicity.

Bibleland, Calimesa, California, 1989

Elk Herd at First Citizen's Bank, Bozeman, Montana, 1988
Wire mesh animals by Jim Dolen proliferate in Bozeman.
(Another noteworthy herd can be found at the airport.)

Condominium Construction, Westwood, California, 1989

Officer West at Dewey's Service, Dewey Bridge & Rte. 128, Utah, 1984

Caesar's Palace, Las Vegas, Nevada, 1988
Taken on the night Sugar Ray Leonard fought Don Lalonde, as is clear
from the huge posters of the two boxers hanging on each side of the statue.

15

Mural on Power Station, New Brunswick, New Jersey, 1985
The power station was demolished shortly after this photograph was taken.
The area is now a park adjoining the Johnson & Johnson headquarters.

16

No Man's Land, Philadelphia, Pennsylvania, 1979

Cabazon, California, 1989
These dinosaurs were built by Claude Bell and were made from concrete and
steel left over from Interstate 10, which runs through Cabazon. Bell was in-
spired to do this work by Lucy the Elephant of Atlantic City (see page 68).

Castle Motors, Reno, Nevada, 1989

Las Vegas, Nevada, 1988

Football Shed for Lawnmowers and Shovels off Interstate 95, Delaware, 1989

Bill Rerria, Veteran's Day Parade, Yuma, Arizona, 1986
The Shriner motor brigades are famous for their precision driving
maneuvers, which they execute in parades throughout America.

Jack Rabbit Trading Post, Rte. 40, Arizona, 1989
Rte. 40 is the interstate that superseded the original Rte. 66.

Seemsville, Pennsylvania, 1989
B. C. Lerch built his little house during the Depression when there wasn't
any work. The house was completely furnished and electrified.

Crayola House, Providence, Rhode Island, 1989

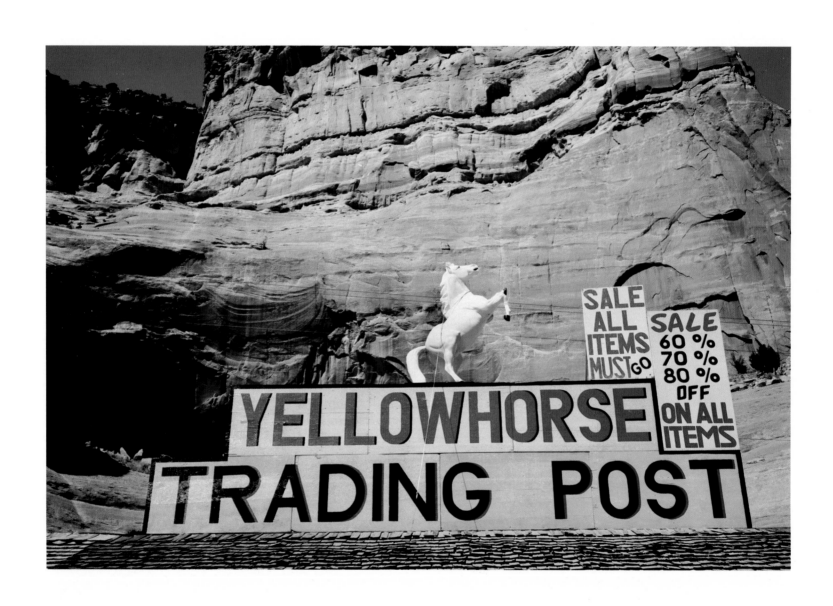

Yellowhorse Trading Post, Lupton, Arizona, 1989

Salt Lake City, Utah, 1988

Hat 'n' Boots Texaco, Seattle, Washington, 1989
The boots were rest rooms.

Motel Ventilator, Holbrook, Arizona, 1989

Indian City Exxon, Rte. 40, Arizona, 1989

33

Paddlewheel Casino, Las Vegas, Nevada, 1988

Mural, Boston, Massachusetts, 1989
Richard Haas painted this mural at 31 Milk Street.

Inflating Spider Man for the Macy's Thanksgiving Day Parade,
New York, New York, 1988

Tempura Store, Los Angeles, California, 1989

Happy Chef, Adrian, Nebraska, 1988

Christine's, Penndel, Pennsylvania, 1984
The Super G Constellation is a cocktail lounge.

Leaning Tower YMCA, Niles, Illinois, 1988
This leaning tower is a water tower.

United Equipment, Turlock, California, 1989
Bulldozer is a two-story office building complete with second-floor
porch for outdoor lunch breaks. The design of the building
is based on a Matchbox toy.

Motel, Winslow, Arizona, 1989

Angelfish, Key Largo, Florida, 1988
A tropical Christmas decoration.

Zippo Lighter Factory, Bradford, Pennsylvania, 1989
The lighter's flame flickers at night and is visible for miles around.

Mormon Temple, Portland, Oregon, 1989

Lincoln's Toe Truck, Seattle, Washington, 1989

51

Vienna, Virginia, 1986

Luckenbaugh's Gift Shop, Paradise, Pennsylvania, 1989
Paradise is in the heart of Pennsylvania Dutch country.

Siperstein Paint Store, Wall, New Jersey, 1989

A Scale Model of the Original USS *Arizona* Sunk at Pearl Harbor,
Philadelphia, Pennsylvania, 1986

Triceratops, Dinosaur, Colorado, 1988
In this Colorado town even the streets are named after dinosaurs.

Hogan, Mancos Valley, Colorado, 1989

Tornado Damage and Insurance, Smyrna, Delaware, 1988

Hilltop Memorial Church, Mexico, New York, 1989
Eleanor Horning became caretaker of this miniature of the real
Hilltop Church when it was moved to her yard.

London Bridge, Lake Havasu City, Arizona, 1989

Wee Kirk o' the Heather Wedding Chapel, Las Vegas, Nevada, 1988

Seattle, Washington, 1989

The Burger that Ate L.A., Los Angeles, California, 1989
Designed and owned by David Alderman and located at Melrose and Stanley.

The Post Bulletins Practicing at Graham Park, Rochester, Minnesota, 1988

Bob & Daisy's South Entrance Motel and Amusement Park,
Midland, Oregon, 1989

Lucy, Margate, New Jersey, 1987
Built in 1883 by James V. Lafferty, Lucy has served a variety of purposes,
from house to hotel to its current state as museum.

Freeway Diesel, Yucca, Arizona, 1989

Places of Learning, Orlando, Florida, 1989

East Los Angeles, California, 1989

Whole Body Counter, Environmental Protection Agency,
Las Vegas, Nevada, 1988
The EPA maintains several of these counters to monitor forty families
for radiation. (Las Vegas is 65 miles from the Nevada Test Site
where atomic bombs are detonated.)

Hallam, Pennsylvania, 1989
Now in hope of funds for restoration, the shoe house was built in the 1930s
by Haines the Shoe Wizard, a discount-store merchant.

Wilshire and Western Avenues, Los Angeles, California, 1989

Three Wise Men, Abington, Pennsylvania, 1979

Rte. 15, Gettysburg, Pennsylvania, 1986
Alan Paulson erected this sampling of wrecks to illustrate to the Department
of Transportation that Rte. 15 needed to be widened. The road
is now four lanes, though the sculpture is gone.

77

Safetyville, Sacramento, California, 1989
Safetyville is a one-third scale model of Sacramento. It is used to
teach children the rules of the road.

Raynham, Massachusetts, 1989

Daytona Beach, Florida, 1989

Sea Missile Motel, Coca Beach, Florida, 1989

Providence, Rhode Island, 1989

Magic World, Pigeon Forge, Tennessee, 1986

Albert the Bull, Audubon, Iowa, 1988
Built in 1964 as a monument to cattlemen and named after
local bank vice president Albert Cruise.

Washington & Broadway, Los Angeles, California, 1989

Las Vegas, Nevada, 1989

Organ, New Mexico, 1986

Milwaukie, Oregon, 1989
Art Lacey flew this B-17 from Oklahoma after purchasing it for his
gas station–restaurant complex. He also collects guns.

Randy's Donuts, Inglewood, California, 1989
Regular customers, Brian Boyd and Robert Pesqueira.

Thunderbird Motel, Mitchell, South Dakota, 1988

Parade, Philadelphia, Pennsylvania, 1988

Wigwam Motel #7, San Bernadino, California, 1989

Bob's Java Jive, Tacoma, Washington, 1989

Daytona Beach, Florida, 1989
Daytona Beach is famous for its "Bike Week."

Des Moines, Iowa, 1988

Rte. 64 west of Rte. 89, Arizona, 1986

A Note on the Type

The text of this book was set in a digitized version of Bembo, a well-known Monotype face. Named for Pietro Bembo, the celebrated Renaissance writer and humanist scholar who was made a cardinal and served as secretary to Pope Leo X, the original cutting of Bembo was made by Francesco Griffo of Bologna only a few years after Columbus discovered America.

Sturdy, well-balanced, and finely proportioned, Bembo is a face of rare beauty, extremely legible in all of its sizes.

Composed by New England Typographic Service, Inc.,
Bloomfield, Connecticut

Separations by Accent on Color,
Hauppauge, New York

Printed and bound by Worzalla Publishing Co.,
Stevens Point, Wisconsin

Designed by Iris Weinstein